Bread Recipes Artisan Bread Cookbook

MARIA SOBININA

BRILLIANTkitchenideas.com

Copyright © 2019 MARIA SOBININA
BRILLIANT kitchen ideas

All rights reserved.

ISBN: 9781097868629

DEDICATION

This book is dedicated to my beautiful family and friends, as well as to you, my reader. I am happy to share the amazing joy of preparing healthy meals with you.

MARIA XOXO

Table of Contents

Basic French Bread   5

Potato Bread   8

Sweet Potato Bread   10

Whole Wheat Bread   14

Rye Bread   17

Basic Artisan Bread   21

Zucchini Bread   25

Pumpkin Bread   27

Pumpkin Yeast Bread   29

Wild Rice Bread   32

Whole Wheat Zucchini Bread   35

Basic Wheat Bread   37

Dates & Nuts Bread   40

Mushrooms Bread   43

Potato Mushroom Bread   45

Olive Bread   49

Strawberry Nut Bread   52

Plum Bread   55

Italian Bread   58

Banana Nut Bread   61

Banana Chocolate Chip Bread   63

Blueberry Crumble Bread   66

Carrot Walnut Bread   70

Almond Flour Banana Bread   73

Almond Flour Coconut Bread   75

Almond Flour Pumpkin Bread   77

Coconut Flour Banana Bread   80

Coconut Flour Pumpkin Bread   82

MARIA SOBININA   BRILLIANTkitchenideas.com

Basic French Bread

Basic French Bread

INGREDIENTS:

6 Cups **Flour**, all-purpose

2 ½ Cup **Water**, warm

2 ¼ Tablespoons **Olive oil**, cold pressed, unrefined

1 ½ teaspoons **Sugar**, cane, white

1 tablespoon **Yeast**, dry, active

2 teaspoons **Salt**, fine, sea

EQUIPMENT:

Stand mixer fitted with the dough hook, Small mixing bowl, Baking tray, Parchment paper, Cooling racks, Plastic wrap (optional).

PREPARATION:

Step 1: In a small mixing bowl add dry yeast and two tablespoons of warm water. Set aside on a countertop for 3-5 minutes to foam.

Step 2: Transfer the yeast water into a bowl of the stand mixer. Add salt, sugar, olive oil and half of the flour. Start mixing on medium-low speed and slowly add the rest of the flour. If the dough is sticking to the sides of the bowl, scrape it with a spatula. The dough will soon start forming a sturdy but soft ball.

Step 3: Leave the dough ball in the mixer and cover with a lid. Set aside for 10 minutes to rise. After 10 minutes beat with a dough hook for 30-45 seconds and set aside for another 10 minutes.

Repeat four more times.

Alternatively, you can leave the dough in the bowl, cover with a plastic wrap and set aside in a warm place for approximately one hour. The dough should double in size.

Step 4: Transfer the dough into a lightly floured surface. Knead it with hands for 1-2 minutes. Cut the dough in half. Shape each half into a loaf.

Step 5: Pre-heat the oven to 375°F. Line the baking tray with parchment paper. Place the loaves into the baking tray.

Bake at 375° for 30-35 minutes or until it becomes golden brown and baked through.

Transfer onto the cooling racks and let it cool.

Basic French Bread will keep for one week in a fridge or up to one month in a freezer.

Potato Bread

Potato Bread

INGREDIENTS:

5 Cups **Flour**, all-purpose

12 Oz **Potato**, boiled

2 ½ Cup **Milk**, warm

2 ¼ Tablespoons **Olive oil**, cold pressed, unrefined

1 ½ teaspoons **Sugar**, cane, white

1 ¼ tablespoon **Yeast**, dry, active

2 teaspoons **Salt**, fine, sea

EQUIPMENT:

Stand mixer fitted with the dough hook, Small and medium mixing bowls, Potato masher, Whisk, Plastic wrap. Two loaf baking trays, Cooling racks.

PREPARATION:

Step 1: In a small mixing bowl add dry yeast and two tablespoons of warm milk. Set aside on a countertop for 3-5 minutes to foam.

Remove skin from the boiled potato. Place the skinned potato into a medium mixing bowl and mash with a masher. Whisk in warm milk.

Add salt, yeast, olive oil, and sugar. Whisk to incorporate.

Whisk in two cups of flour.

Step 2: Transfer the mixture into the bowl of a stand mixer. Start mixing on medium-low speed and slowly add the rest of the flour. If the dough is sticking to the sides of the bowl, scrape it with a spatula. The dough will soon start forming a sturdy but soft ball.

Step 3: Leave the dough in the bowl, cover with a plastic wrap and set aside in a warm place for approximately two hours. The dough should at least double in size.

Step 4: Transfer the dough into lightly floured surface. Knead the dough with hands for 1-2 minutes.

Cut the dough in half. Shape each half into a loaf. Place the loaves into two greased baking trays. Push down with your fingers. Set aside, cover with a plastic wrap and let the dough rise again.

Step 5: Pre-heat the oven to 350°F. Place the loaf trays into the oven.

Bake at 350° for 30-35 minutes or until it becomes golden brown and baked through.

Transfer onto the cooling racks and let it cool.

Potato Bread will keep for one week in a fridge or up to one month in a freezer.

Sweet Potato Bread

INGREDIENTS:

5 Cups **Flour**, all-purpose

12 Oz **Sweet potato**, boiled

2 ½ Cup **Milk**, warm

1 Cup **Pistachios**, chopped

½ Cup **Cranberries**, dried

½ Cup **Raisins**, golden, dried

2 ¼ Tablespoons **Olive oil**, cold pressed, unrefined

1 ½ teaspoons **Sugar**, cane, white

1 ¼ tablespoon **Yeast**, dry, active

2 teaspoons **Salt**, fine, sea

¼ teaspoon **Cinnamon**, powder

EQUIPMENT:

Stand mixer fitted with the dough hook, Small and medium mixing bowls, Potato masher, Whisk, Plastic wrap, Two loaf baking trays, Cooling racks.

PREPARATION:

Step 1: In a small mixing bowl add dry yeast and two

tablespoons of warm milk. Set aside on a countertop for 3-5 minutes to foam.

Remove skin from the boiled sweet potatoes. Place the skinned potatoes into a medium mixing bowl and mash with a masher. Whisk in warm milk.

Add salt, yeast, olive oil, cinnamon, and sugar. Whisk to incorporate.

Whisk in two cups of flour, pistachios, raisins, and cranberries.

Step 2: Transfer the mixture into the bowl of a stand mixer. Start mixing on medium-low speed and slowly add the rest of the flour. If the dough is sticking to the sides of the bowl, scrape it with a spatula. The dough will soon start forming a sturdy but soft ball.

Step 3: Leave the dough in the bowl, cover with a plastic wrap and set aside in a warm place for approximately two hours. The dough should at least double in size.

Step 4: Transfer the dough into lightly floured surface. Knead the dough with hands for 1-2 minutes.

Cut the dough in half. Shape each half into a loaf. Place the loaves into two greased baking trays. Push down with your fingers. Set aside, cover with a plastic wrap and let the dough rise again.

Step 5: Pre-heat the oven to 360°F. Place the loaf trays into the oven.

Bake at 360° for 30-35 minutes or until it becomes golden brown and baked through.

Transfer onto the cooling racks and let it cool.

Sweet Potato Bread will keep for one week in a fridge or up to one month in a freezer.

Whole Wheat Brea

Whole Wheat Bread

INGREDIENTS:

6 Cups **Flour**, wheat

2 ½ Cup **Water**, warm

½ Cup **Milk**, dried, non-fat

2 ¼ Tablespoons **Olive oil**, cold pressed, unrefined

2 Tablespoons **Molasses**

1 tablespoon **Yeast**, dry, active

2 teaspoons **Salt**, fine, sea

EQUIPMENT:

Stand mixer fitted with the dough hook, Small mixing bowl, Baking tray, Parchment paper, Cooling racks, Plastic wrap Two loaf baking trays, Cooling racks.

PREPARATION:

Step 1: In a small mixing bowl add dry yeast and two tablespoons of warm water. Set aside on a countertop for 3-5 minutes to foam.

Step 2: Transfer the yeast water into a bowl of the stand mixer. Add salt, dried milk, olive oil, molasses, and half of the flour. Start mixing on medium-low speed and slowly add the rest of the flour. If the dough is sticking to the sides of the bowl, scrape it with a spatula. The dough will soon start forming a sturdy but soft ball.

Step 3: Leave the dough in the bowl, cover with a plastic wrap and set aside in a warm place for approximately one to two hours, depending on temperature in your kitchen. The dough should increase in size.

Step 4: Transfer the dough into a lightly floured surface. Knead it with hands for 1-2 minutes. Cut the dough in half. Shape each half into a loaf.

Place the loafs into the baking trays. Cover the trays with plastic wrap and set aside to rise for one to two hours.

Step 5: Pre-heat the oven to 350°F. Place the trays into the oven.

Bake at 350° for 35-40 minutes or until it becomes golden brown and baked through.

Transfer onto the cooling racks and let it cool.

Whole Wheat Bread will keep for one week in a fridge or up to one month in a freezer.

MARIA SOBININA   BRILLIANTkitchenideas.com

Rye Bread

Rye Bread

INGREDIENTS:

2 Cups **Flour**, all-purpose

2 Cups **Rye flour**

1 Cup **Water**, warm

2 ¼ Tablespoons **Olive oil**, cold pressed, unrefined

½ Cup **Sugar**, brown

½ Cup **Molasses**

1 teaspoons **Sugar**, cane, white

1 ½ Tablespoon **Yeast**, dry, active

2 teaspoons **Salt**, fine, sea

1 teaspoon **Anise**, seeds, dried

EQUIPMENT:

Stand mixer fitted with the dough hook, Medium and large mixing bowls, (Pizza) Baking stone, Cooling racks, Plastic wrap (optional).

PREPARATION:

Step 1: In a large mixing bowl, combine flour, rye

flour, sugar, brown sugar, yeast, anise, and salt. Mix with a spatula to combine. Add water, olive oil, molasses and mix with the spatula to incorporate. Cover the bowl with a plastic wrap and set aside at room temperature for 1-2 hours to rise.

Step 2: After the dough has risen, transfer it onto work surface dusted with flour. Knead the dough for 1-2 minutes, fold the dough in half, and then roll it into a ball.

Step 3: Generously sprinkle the bottom of a medium mixing bowl with flour. Place the dough ball into the mixing bowl and cover it with a plastic wrap. Set it aside for two hour to rise.

Step 4: Transfer the dough into a lightly floured surface. Knead it with hands for 1-2 minutes. Cut the dough in half. Shape each half into a loaf. Cut several parallel lines on top.

Step 5: Place the baking stone into the cold oven. Pre-heat the oven and the baking stone to 375°F. Place the loaves into the baking stone.

Bake at 375° for 30-35 minutes or until it becomes golden brown and baked through.

Transfer onto the cooling racks and let it cool.

Olive Bread will keep for one week in a fridge or up to one month in a freezer.

Basic Artisan Bread

Basic Artisan Bread

INGREDIENTS:

6 Cups **Flour**, all-purpose

2 ½ Cup **Water**, warm

2 ¼ Tablespoons **Olive oil**, cold pressed, unrefined

1 ½ teaspoons **Sugar**, cane, white

1 tablespoon **Yeast**, dry, active

2 teaspoons **Salt**, fine, sea

1 teaspoon **Rosemary**, dried

1 teaspoon **Sage**, dried

EQUIPMENT:

Stand mixer fitted with the dough hook, Medium and large mixing bowls, Dutch oven, Heat-proof gloves, Parchment paper, Cooling racks, Plastic wrap (optional).

PREPARATION:

Step 1: In a large mixing bowl, combine flour, yeast, herbs, and salt. Mix with a spatula to combine. Add water and mix with the spatula to incorporate. Cover the bowl with a plastic wrap and set aside at room temperature overnight or up to 24 hours.

Step 2: After the dough has risen, transfer it onto work surface dusted with flour. Knead the dough for 1-2 minutes, fold the dough in half, and then roll it into a ball.

Step 3: Generously sprinkle the bottom of a medium mixing bowl with flour. Place the dough ball into the mixing bowl and cover it with a plastic wrap. Set it aside for two hour to rise.

Step 4: Preheat the oven to 425°F. Place the Dutch oven and the lead into the oven to preheat.

Step 5: Remove the Dutch oven from the oven, using the heat-proof gloves. Careful, it will be very hot.

Place the dough ball in to the hot Dutch oven, cover with the lid and place back into the oven.

Bake for 30 minutes. Remove the lid and bake for another 15 minutes until the crust will turn golden brown.

Step 6: Once ready, remove from the Dutch oven, transfer into cooling racks and let to cool completely.

Basic Artisan Bread will keep for one week in a fridge or up to one month in a freezer.

Zucchini Bread

Zucchini Bread

INGREDIENTS:

3 Cups **Flour**, all-purpose

3 Cups **Zucchini**, grated

2 **Eggs**, large

2 ¼ Tablespoons **Olive oil**, cold pressed, unrefined

1 ½ Cup **Sugar**, cane, white

1 Cup **Pecans**, chopped

2 teaspoons **Salt**, fine, sea

1 teaspoon **Baking powder**

1 teaspoon **Vanilla**, extract, pure

¼ teaspoon **Cinnamon**, powder

EQUIPMENT:

Large and medium mixing bowls, Grater, Whisk, Spatula, Two loaf baking trays, Cooling racks.

PREPARATION:

Step 1: Preheat the oven to 355°F. Grease the loaf baking trays. Drain the excess water from zucchinis.

Step 2: In a medium mixing bowl combine all dry

ingredients: flour, sugar, pecans, salt, baking powder and cinnamon. Whisk together.

Step 3: In a large mixing bowl combine all wet ingredients: zucchinis, eggs, olive oil, and vanilla. Whisk together.

Step 4: Combine dry and wet ingredients in the large bowl. Fold in with a spatula to incorporate all together.

Step 5: Distribute the batter between two greased trays. Bake for 45-50 minutes at 355°F or until the wooden tester comes out clean.

Transfer onto the cooling racks and let it cool.

Zucchini Bread will keep for one week in a fridge or up to one month in a freezer.

Pumpkin Bread

INGREDIENTS:

3 Cups **Flour**, all-purpose

3 Cups **Pumpkin**, cubed

2 **Eggs**, large

2 ¼ Tablespoons **Olive oil**, cold pressed, unrefined

2 Cups **Molasses**

1 Cup **Pistachios**, chopped

1 Cup **Cranberries**, dried

2 teaspoons **Salt**, fine, sea

1 teaspoon **Baking powder**

1 teaspoon **Vanilla**, extract, pure

¼ teaspoon **Cinnamon**, powder

¼ teaspoon **Nutmeg**, powder

EQUIPMENT:

Medium saucepan, Masher, Large, medium, and small mixing bowls, Grater, Whisk, Spatula, Two loaf baking trays, Cooling racks.

PREPARATION:

Step 1: Place pumpkin into medium saucepan and boil it until it becomes soft. Once the pumpkin is ready, place it in a small mixing bowl and mash it with a masher.

Step 2: Preheat the oven to 355°F. Grease the loaf baking trays.

Step 3: In a medium mixing bowl combine all dry ingredients: flour, pistachios, cranberry, salt, baking powder, nutmeg, and cinnamon. Whisk together.

Step 4: In a large mixing bowl combine all wet ingredients: pumpkin, molasses, eggs, olive oil, and vanilla. Whisk together.

Step 5: Combine dry and wet ingredients in the large bowl. Fold in with a spatula to incorporate all together.

Step 6: Distribute the batter between two greased trays. Bake for 45-50 minutes at 355°F or until the wooden tester comes out clean.

Transfer onto the cooling racks and let it cool.

Pumpkin Bread will keep for one week in a fridge or up to one month in a freezer.

Pumpkin Yeast Bread

INGREDIENTS:

6 Cups **Flour**, all-purpose

2 Cups **Pumpkin**, pureed

2 **Eggs**, large

½ Cup **Milk**, warm

2 ¼ Tablespoons **Olive oil**, cold pressed, unrefined

1 Cup **Molasses**

2 tablespoon **Yeast**, dry, active

2 teaspoons **Salt**, fine, sea

½ teaspoon **Cinnamon**, powder

EQUIPMENT:

Stand mixer fitted with the dough hook, Masher, Small mixing bowl, Baking tray, Parchment paper, Cooling racks, Plastic wrap.

PREPARATION:

Step 1: In a small mixing bowl add dry yeast and warm milk. Set aside on a countertop for 3-5 minutes to foam.

Boil and puree pumpkin with a masher.

Step 2: Transfer the yeast milk into a bowl of the stand mixer. Add pureed pumpkin, molasses, eggs, olive oil and half of the flour. Start mixing on medium-low speed and slowly add the rest of the flour. If the dough is sticking to the sides of the bowl, scrape it with a spatula. The dough will soon start forming a sturdy but soft ball.

Step 3: Leave the dough in the bowl, cover with a plastic wrap and set aside in a warm place for approximately one hour. The dough should double in size.

Step 4: Transfer the dough into a lightly floured surface. Knead it with hands for 1-2 minutes. Cut the dough in half. Shape each half into a loaf.

Step 5: Preheat the oven to 355°F. Grease the loaf baking trays.

Distribute the batter between two greased trays. Bake for 40-45 minutes Transfer onto the cooling racks and let it cool.

Pumpkin Yeast Bread will keep for one week in a fridge or up to one month in a freezer.

Wild Rice Bread

Wild Rice Bread

INGREDIENTS:

3 Cups **Bread flour,** unbleached

1 Cup **Flour,** whole wheat

2 Cups **Rice,** wild, cooked

½ Cup **Sourdough starter**, ripe

1 ½ Cup **Water**, warm

1 Cup **Pistachios**, chopped

1 Cup **Cranberries**, dried

1 ¼ tablespoon **Yeast**, dry, active

1 ½ teaspoons **Maple syrup**

2 teaspoons **Salt**, fine, sea

EQUIPMENT:

Stand mixer fitted with the paddle attachment and dough hook, Large mixing bowl, Plastic wrap. Two loaf baking trays, Cooling racks.

PREPARATION:

Step 1: In a bowl of a stand mixer add sourdough starter, water, yeast, maple syrup and whole wheat flour. Beat with the paddle attachment until smooth. Cover the bowl with a plastic wrap and let it sit for 1 – 2 hours until the dough becomes bubbly.

Step 2: Add salt and gradually beat in the bread flour. Remove the paddle attachment and install a dough hook.

Knead for 8-10 minutes. Add rice, pistachios, and cranberries. Knead to incorporate.

Step 3: Transfer the dough into a large bowl sprinkled with flour. Cover with a plastic wrap and set aside to side for 1-2 hours.

Step 4: Transfer the dough into lightly floured surface. Deflate and knead the dough with hands for 1-2 minutes.

Cut the dough in half. Shape each half into a loaf. Place the loaves into two greased baking trays. Push down with your fingers. Set aside, cover with a plastic wrap and let the dough rise again. This will take approximately one hour.

Step 5: Pre-heat the oven to 365°F. Place the loaf trays into the oven.

Bake at 365° for 40-45 minutes or until it becomes golden brown and baked through.

Transfer onto the cooling racks and let it cool.

Wild Rice Bread will keep for one week in a fridge or up to one month in a freezer.

Whole Wheat Zucchini Bread

INGREDIENTS:

1 ½ Cup **Flour**, all-purpose

1 ½ Cup **Flour**, whole wheat

3 Cups **Zucchini**, grated

2 **Eggs**, large

1 ¼ Tablespoons **Olive oil**, cold pressed, unrefined

½ Cup **Sugar**, brown

½ Cup **Molasses**

1 Cup **Raisins,** golden

½ Cup **Pecans**, chopped

½ Cup **Walnuts**, chopped

½ Cup **Pistachios**, chopped

2 teaspoons **Salt**, fine, sea

1 teaspoon **Baking powder**

1 teaspoon **Vanilla**, extract, pure

¼ teaspoon **Cinnamon**, powder

EQUIPMENT:

Large and medium mixing bowls, Grater, Whisk, Spatula, Two loaf baking trays, Cooling racks.

PREPARATION:

Step 1: Preheat the oven to 355°F. Grease the loaf baking trays. Drain the excess water from zucchinis.

Step 2: In a medium mixing bowl combine all dry ingredients: flour, wheat flour, sugar, pecans, walnuts, pistachios, cranberries, raisins, salt, baking powder and cinnamon. Whisk together.

Step 3: In a large mixing bowl combine all wet ingredients: zucchinis, molasses, eggs, olive oil, and vanilla. Whisk together.

Step 4: Combine dry and wet ingredients in the large bowl. Fold in with a spatula to incorporate all together.

Step 5: Distribute the batter between two greased trays. Bake for 45-50 minutes at 355°F or until the wooden tester comes out clean.

Transfer onto the cooling racks and let it cool.

Whole Wheat Zucchini Bread will keep for one week in a fridge or up to one month in a freezer.

Basic Wheat Bread

INGREDIENTS:

3 Cups **Flour**, all-purpose

3 Cups **Flour**, whole wheat

2 Tablespoons **Butter**, melted, unsalted

1 ½ Cup **Molasses**

1 ¼ tablespoon **Yeast**, dry, active

2 teaspoons **Salt**, fine, sea

EQUIPMENT:

Large and medium mixing bowls, Spatula, Two loaf baking trays, Plastic wrap, Cooling racks.

PREPARATION:

Step 1: In a large bowl combine warm water, yeast and ½ of molasses. Mix in all all-purpose flour. Set aside for 30-40 minutes or until it becomes bubbly.

Step 2: Once the mixture becomes bubbly, add the rest of molasses, melted butter, salt and wheat flour. Mix with hands.

Step 3: Transfer the batter onto floured surface. Knead the batter with hands until it becomes firm but still sticky. You may need to add more wheat flour to get to the desired consistency.

Step 4: Place into a greased bowl. Cover with a plastic wrap. Set aside for 1-2 hours to rise.

Step 5: Preheat the oven to 355°F. Grease the loaf baking trays.

Distribute the batter between two greased trays. Bake for 25 - 30 minutes at 355°F or until the wooden tester comes out clean.

Transfer onto the cooling racks and let it cool.

Whole Wheat Bread will keep for one week in a fridge or up to one month in a freezer.

Dates & Nuts Bread

Dates & Nuts Bread

INGREDIENTS:

2 Cups **Flour**, all-purpose

2 Cups **Dates**, chopped

¾ Cup **Water**, warm

½ Cup **Cocoa**, powder, unsweetened

2 **Eggs**, large

2 Tablespoons **Olive oil**, cold pressed, unrefined

2 Tablespoons **Butter**, softened

1 Cup **Molasses**

½ Cup **Sugar**, brown

½ Cup **Macadamia nuts**, chopped

½ Cup **Walnuts**, chopped

½ Cup **Hazelnuts**, chopped

1 Tablespoon **Brandy**

2 teaspoons **Salt**, fine, sea

1 teaspoon **Baking powder**

1 teaspoon **Vanilla**, extract, pure

EQUIPMENT:

Large and medium mixing bowls, Whisk, Spatula, Two loaf baking trays, Cooling racks.

PREPARATION:

Step 1: Preheat the oven to 355°F. Grease the loaf baking trays.

Step 2: In a medium mixing bowl combine all dry ingredients: flour, brown sugar, cocoa powder, dates, macadamia nuts, walnuts, hazelnuts, salt, and baking powder. Whisk together.

Step 3: In a large mixing bowl combine all wet ingredients: water, molasses, eggs, olive oil, and butter. Whisk together.

Step 4: Combine dry and wet ingredients in the large bowl. Add vanilla extract and brandy. Fold in with a spatula to incorporate all together.

Step 5: Distribute the batter between two greased trays. Bake for 45-50 minutes at 355°F or until the wooden tester comes out clean.

Transfer onto the cooling racks and let it cool.

Dates & Nuts Bread will keep for one week in a fridge or up to one month in a freezer.

Mushroom Bread

Mushrooms Bread

INGREDIENTS:

3 Cups **Flour**, all-purpose

4 Cups **Mushrooms**, white, coarsely chopped

2 Cups **Onions**, yellow, chopped

2 Tablespoons **Butter,** unsalted

2 **Eggs**, large

½ Cup **Water**, warm

2 ¼ Tablespoons **Olive oil**, cold pressed, unrefined

½ Tablespoon **Sugar**, brown

2 teaspoons **Salt**, fine, sea

1 teaspoon **Baking powder**

1 teaspoon **Vanilla**, extract, pure

¼ teaspoon **Nutmeg**, powder

¼ teaspoon **Black pepper**, powder

EQUIPMENT:

Medium skillet, Large, medium, and small mixing bowls, Grater, Whisk, Spatula, Two loaf baking trays, Cooling racks.

PREPARATION:

Step 1: Add butter into a skillet and heat it over medium heat. Place mushrooms and onions into the skillet. Fry it on medium heat for 5-7 minutes until mushrooms become fragrant. Set aside.

Step 2: Preheat the oven to 355°F. Grease the loaf baking trays.

Step 3: In a medium mixing bowl combine all dry ingredients: flour, sugar, salt, baking powder, nutmeg, and black pepper. Whisk together.

Step 4: In a large mixing bowl combine all wet ingredients: water, mushrooms, eggs, olive oil, and vanilla. Whisk together.

Step 5: Combine dry and wet ingredients in the large bowl. Fold in with a spatula to incorporate all together. If the mixture is too dry add a little bit more water.

Step 6: Distribute the batter between two greased trays. Bake for 45-50 minutes at 355°F or until the wooden tester comes out clean.

Transfer onto the cooling racks and let it cool.

Mushroom Bread will keep for one week in a fridge or up to one month in a freezer.

Potato Mushroom Bread

INGREDIENTS:

5 Cups **Flour**, all-purpose

6 Oz **Potato**, boiled

6 Oz **Mushrooms**, white chopped

2 Tablespoons **Butter,** unsalted

2 ½ Cup **Milk**, warm

2 ¼ Tablespoons **Olive oil**, cold pressed, unrefined

1 ½ teaspoons **Sugar**, cane, white

1 ¼ tablespoon **Yeast**, dry, active

2 teaspoons **Salt**, fine, sea

EQUIPMENT:

Medium skillet, Stand mixer fitted with the dough hook, Small and medium mixing bowls, Potato masher, Whisk, Plastic wrap. Two loaf baking trays, Cooling racks.

PREPARATION:

Step 1: Add butter into a skillet and heat it over medium heat. Place mushrooms into the skillet. Fry it on medium heat for 5-7 minutes until mushrooms become fragrant. Set aside.

Step 2: In a small mixing bowl add dry yeast and two tablespoons of warm milk. Set aside on a countertop for 3-5 minutes to foam.

Remove skin from the boiled potato. Place the skinned potato into a medium mixing bowl and mash with a masher. Whisk in warm milk.

Add salt, yeast, olive oil, and sugar. Whisk to incorporate.

Whisk in two cups of flour.

Step 3: Transfer the mixture into the bowl of a stand mixer. Start mixing on medium-low speed and slowly add the rest of the flour. If the dough is sticking to the sides of the bowl, scrape it with a spatula. The dough will soon start forming a sturdy but soft ball.

Step 4: Leave the dough in the bowl, cover with a plastic wrap and set aside in a warm place for approximately two hours. The dough should at least double in size.

Step 5: Transfer the dough into lightly floured surface. Knead the dough with hands for 1-2 minutes. Fold in mushrooms.

Cut the dough in half. Shape each half into a loaf. Place the loaves into two greased baking trays. Push down with your fingers. Set aside, cover with a plastic wrap and let the dough rise again.

Step 6: Pre-heat the oven to 350°F. Place the loaf trays into the oven.

Bake at 350° for 30-35 minutes or until it becomes golden brown and baked through.

Transfer onto the cooling racks and let it cool.

Potato Mushroom Bread will keep for one week in a fridge or up to one month in a freezer.

Olive Bread

Olive Bread

INGREDIENTS:

4 Cups **Flour**, all-purpose

1 ¾ Cup **Olives**, black, pitted

1 ¼ Cup **Water**, warm

2 ¼ Tablespoons **Olive oil**, cold pressed, unrefined

1 ½ teaspoons **Sugar**, cane, white

3/4 Tablespoon **Yeast**, dry, active

2 teaspoons **Salt**, fine, sea

1 teaspoon **Rosemary**, dried

EQUIPMENT:

Stand mixer fitted with the dough hook, Medium and large mixing bowls, Two baking trays, Parchment paper, Cooling racks, Plastic wrap (optional).

PREPARATION:

Step 1: In a large mixing bowl, combine flour, olives, yeast, herbs, and salt. Mix with a spatula to combine. Add water, olive oil and mix with the spatula to incorporate. Cover the bowl with a plastic wrap and set aside at room temperature for 1-2 hours to rise.

Step 2: After the dough has risen, transfer it onto work surface dusted with flour. Knead the dough for 1-2 minutes, fold the dough in half, and then roll it into a ball.

Step 3: Generously sprinkle the bottom of a medium mixing bowl with flour. Place the dough ball into the mixing bowl and cover it with a plastic wrap. Set it aside for two hour to rise.

Step 4: Transfer the dough into a lightly floured surface. Knead it with hands for 1-2 minutes. Cut the dough in half. Shape each half into a loaf.

Step 5: Pre-heat the oven to 375°F. Line the baking trays with parchment paper. Place the loaves into the baking trays.

Bake at 375° for 30-35 minutes or until it becomes golden brown and baked through.

Transfer onto the cooling racks and let it cool.

Olive Bread will keep for one week in a fridge or up to one month in a freezer.

Strawberry Nut Bread

Strawberry Nut Bread

INGREDIENTS:

2 Cups **Flour**, all-purpose

2 Cups **Strawberries**, chopped

¾ Cup **Water**, warm

2 **Eggs**, large

2 Tablespoons **Olive oil**, cold pressed, unrefined

2 Tablespoons **Butter**, softened

1 Cup **Molasses**

½ Cup **Sugar**, brown

½ Cup **Macadamia nuts**, chopped

½ Cup **Walnuts**, chopped

2 teaspoons **Salt**, fine, sea

1 teaspoon **Baking powder**

1 teaspoon **Vanilla**, extract, pure

EQUIPMENT:

Large and medium mixing bowls, Grater, Whisk, Spatula, Two loaf baking trays, Cooling racks.

PREPARATION:

Step 1: Preheat the oven to 355°F. Grease the loaf baking trays.

Step 2: In a medium mixing bowl combine all dry ingredients: flour, brown sugar, macadamia nuts, walnuts, salt, and baking powder. Whisk together.

Step 3: In a large mixing bowl combine all wet ingredients: strawberries, water, molasses, eggs, olive oil, and butter. Whisk together.

Step 4: Combine dry and wet ingredients in the large bowl. Add vanilla extract. Fold in the ingredients with a spatula to incorporate all together.

Step 5: Distribute the batter between two greased trays. Bake for 45-50 minutes at 355°F or until the wooden tester comes out clean.

Transfer onto the cooling racks and let it cool.

Strawberry Nut Bread will keep for one week in a fridge or up to one month in a freezer.

Plum Bread

Plum Bread

INGREDIENTS:

2 Cups **Flour**, all-purpose

2 Cups **Plums**, dried, pitted, chopped

1 Cup **Raisins**, brown

1 Cup **Walnuts**, chopped

¾ Cup **Water**, warm

2 **Eggs**, large

2 ½ Tablespoons **Olive oil**, cold pressed, unrefined

1 Cup **Molasses**

½ Cup **Sugar**, brown

2 teaspoons **Salt**, fine, sea

1 teaspoon **Baking powder**

1 teaspoon **Vanilla**, extract, pure

¼ teaspoon **Nutmeg**, powder

EQUIPMENT:

Large and medium mixing bowls, Grater, Whisk, Spatula, Two loaf baking trays, Cooling racks.

PREPARATION:

Step 1: Preheat the oven to 355°F. Grease the loaf baking trays.

Step 2: In a medium mixing bowl combine all dry ingredients: flour, brown sugar, plums, raisins, walnuts, salt, and baking powder. Whisk together.

Step 3: In a large mixing bowl combine all wet ingredients: water, molasses, eggs, and olive oil. Whisk together.

Step 4: Combine dry and wet ingredients in the large bowl. Add vanilla extract. Fold in the ingredients with a spatula to incorporate all together.

Step 5: Distribute the batter between two greased trays. Bake for 45-50 minutes at 355°F or until the wooden tester comes out clean.

Transfer onto the cooling racks and let it cool.

Plum Bread will keep for one week in a fridge or up to one month in a freezer.

Italian Bread

Italian Bread

INGREDIENTS:

6 Cups **Flour**, all-purpose

2 ¼ Cup **Water**, warm

1 teaspoons **Sugar**, cane, white

1 ¼ tablespoon **Yeast**, dry, active

2 teaspoons **Salt**, fine, sea

EQUIPMENT:

Stand mixer fitted with the dough hook, Small mixing bowl, Baking tray, Kitchen knife, Parchment paper, Cooling racks, Plastic wrap (optional).

PREPARATION:

Step 1: In a small mixing bowl add dry yeast and two tablespoons of warm water. Set aside on a countertop for 3-5 minutes to foam.

Step 2: Transfer the yeast water into a bowl of the stand mixer. Add salt, sugar, and half of the flour. Start mixing on medium-low speed and slowly add the rest of the flour. If the dough is sticking to the sides of the bowl, scrape it with a spatula. The dough will soon start forming a sturdy but soft ball.

Step 3: Leave the dough in the bowl, cover with a plastic wrap and set aside in a warm place for approximately one hour. The dough should double in size.

Step 4: Transfer the dough into a lightly floured surface. Knead it with hands for 1-2 minutes. Cut the dough in half. Shape each half into a loaf. Make four shallow slashes on the top of each loaf with a kitchen knife.

Step 5: Pre-heat the oven to 375°F. Line the baking tray with parchment paper. Place the loaves into the baking tray.

Bake at 375° for 30-35 minutes or until it becomes golden brown and baked through.

Transfer onto the cooling racks and let it cool.

Italian Bread will keep for one week in a fridge or up to one month in a freezer.

Banana Nut Bread

Banana Nut Bread

INGREDIENTS:

3 Cups **Flour**, all-purpose

5 **Bananas**, mashed

2 **Eggs**, large

2 ¼ Tablespoons **Olive oil**, cold pressed, unrefined

1 ½ Cup **Sugar**, brown

1 Cup **Pecans**, chopped

1 Cup **Walnuts**, chopped

1 Cup **Cranberries**, dried

2 teaspoons **Salt**, fine, sea

1 teaspoon **Baking powder**

1 teaspoon **Vanilla**, extract, pure

EQUIPMENT:

Large and medium mixing bowls, Masher, Whisk, Spatula, Two loaf baking trays, Cooling racks.

PREPARATION:

Step 1: Preheat the oven to 355°F. Grease the loaf baking trays. Mash bananas with a masher.

Step 2: In a medium mixing bowl combine all dry ingredients: flour, brown sugar, pecans, walnuts, cranberries, salt, and baking powder. Whisk together.

Step 3: In a large mixing bowl combine all wet ingredients: bananas, eggs, olive oil, and vanilla. Whisk together.

Step 4: Combine dry and wet ingredients in the large bowl. Fold in with a spatula to incorporate all together.

Step 5: Distribute the batter between two greased trays. Bake for 50 - 55 minutes at 355°F or until the wooden tester comes out clean.

Transfer onto the cooling racks and let it cool.

Banana Nut Bread will keep for one week in a fridge or up to one month in a freezer.

Banana Chocolate Chip Bread

INGREDIENTS:

3 Cups **Flour**, all-purpose

5 **Bananas**, mashed

2 **Eggs**, large

2 ¼ Tablespoons **Olive oil**, cold pressed, unrefined

1 ½ Cup **Sugar**, brown

1 Cup **Pecans**, chopped

1 Cup **Chocolate chips**, dark, mini, bakers

2 teaspoons **Salt**, fine, sea

1 teaspoon **Baking powder**

1 teaspoon **Vanilla**, extract, pure

¼ teaspoon **Nutmeg**, powder

EQUIPMENT:

Large and medium mixing bowls, Masher, Whisk, Spatula, Two loaf baking trays, Cooling racks.

PREPARATION:

Step 1: Preheat the oven to 355°F. Grease the loaf baking trays. Mash bananas with a masher.

Step 2: In a medium mixing bowl combine all dry ingredients: flour, brown sugar, pecans, chocolate chips, salt, baking powder, and nutmeg. Whisk together.

Step 3: In a large mixing bowl combine all wet ingredients: bananas, eggs, olive oil, and vanilla. Whisk together.

Step 4: Combine dry and wet ingredients in the large bowl. Fold in with a spatula to incorporate all together.

Step 5: Distribute the batter between two greased trays. Bake for 50 - 55 minutes at 355°F or until the wooden tester comes out clean.

Transfer onto the cooling racks and let it cool.

Banana Chocolate Chip Bread will keep for one week in a fridge or up to one month in a freezer.

Blueberry Crumble Bread

Blueberry Crumble Bread

INGREDIENTS:

FOR THE CRUMBLES:

1 Cup **Flour**, all purpose

1 Cup **Sugar**, granulated

3 Oz **Butter**, unsalted

½ teaspoon **Salt**, sea, fine

FOR THE BREAD:

3 Cups **Flour**, all-purpose

3 Cups **Blueberries**, fresh

2 **Eggs**, large

1 Cup **Milk**, whole

2 ¼ Tablespoons **Olive oil**, cold pressed, unrefined

1 ½ Cup **Sugar**, cane, white

2 teaspoons **Salt**, fine, sea

1 teaspoon **Baking powder**

1 teaspoon **Vanilla**, extract, pure

EQUIPMENT:

One large and two medium mixing bowls, Whisk, Spatula, Two loaf baking trays, Cooling racks.

PREPARATION:

MAKE THE CRUMBLES:

In a medium bowl, combine flour, sugar and butter. Do not over mix. The mixture will be granular.

MAKE THE BREAD BATTER:

Step 1: Preheat the oven to 355°F. Grease the loaf baking trays.

Step 2: In a medium mixing bowl combine all dry ingredients: flour, sugar, salt, baking powder. Whisk together.

Step 3: In a large mixing bowl combine all wet ingredients: milk, eggs, olive oil, and vanilla. Whisk together.

Step 4: Combine dry and wet ingredients in the large bowl. Fold in with a spatula to incorporate all together. Carefully fold in blueberries.

Step 5: Distribute the batter between two greased trays. Spread the crumbles on top of the bread batter.

Bake for 45-50 minutes at 355°F or until the wooden tester comes out clean.

Transfer onto the cooling racks and let it cool.

Blueberry Crumble Bread will keep for one week in a fridge or up to one month in a freezer.

Carrot Walnut Bread

Carrot Walnut Bread

INGREDIENTS:

3 Cups **Flour**, all-purpose

3 Cups **Carrots**, grated

2 **Eggs**, large

2 ¼ Tablespoons **Olive oil**, cold pressed, unrefined

2 Cups **Molasses**

1 Cup **Walnuts**, chopped

1 Cup **Cranberries**, dried

2 teaspoons **Salt**, fine, sea

1 teaspoon **Baking powder**

1 teaspoon **Vanilla**, extract, pure

¼ teaspoon **Ginger**, powder

¼ teaspoon **Nutmeg**, powder

EQUIPMENT:

Grater, Large, medium, and small mixing bowls, Grater, Whisk, Spatula, Two loaf baking trays, Cooling racks.

PREPARATION:

Step 1: Grate carrots into a small bowl. Set aside.

Step 2: Preheat the oven to 355°F. Grease the loaf baking trays.

Step 3: In a medium mixing bowl combine all dry ingredients: flour, walnuts, cranberry, salt, baking powder, nutmeg, and ginger. Whisk together.

Step 4: In a large mixing bowl combine all wet ingredients: carrots, molasses, eggs, olive oil, and vanilla. Whisk together.

Step 5: Combine dry and wet ingredients in the large bowl. Fold in with a spatula to incorporate all together.

Step 6: Distribute the batter between two greased trays. Bake for 45-50 minutes at 355°F or until the wooden tester comes out clean.

Transfer onto the cooling racks and let it cool.

Carrot Walnut Bread will keep for one week in a fridge or up to one month in a freezer.

Almond Flour Banana Bread

Almond Flour Banana Bread

INGREDIENTS:

3 cups **Almond Flour**

2 **Bananas**, ripe, mashed

½ cup **Almond Milk**

¼ cup **Honey**, raw

¼ cup **Olive Oil**, virgin, first cold pressed

4 tablespoons **Water**, hot

2 tablespoons **Flax Seeds**, ground

1 teaspoon **Baking Soda**

1 teaspoon **Vanilla**, extract, pure

¼ teaspoon **Salt,** fine, pink, Himalayan

Cooking Spray for greasing the baking tray

EQUIPMENT:

Rectangular bread baking tray, Stand or hand mixer fitted with the paddle attachment, Measuring cups, Cup, Fork, Wire cooling racks, Parchment paper (optional), Cake decorating piping tips and bags (optional).

PREPARATION:

Step 1: Prepare egg replacement: add flax seeds into a cup and cover it with hot water. Place flax seeds onto a countertop and wait until flax seeds become gelatin-like.

Step 2: Grease the bottom and sides of the baking tray with a cooking spray. Line the bottom of the tray with parchment paper (optional).

Step 3: In a bowl of a stand mixer, mash bananas with a fork. Add flax eggs, almond flour, almond milk, olive oil, honey, baking soda, salt, and vanilla extract. Process everything on low-medium speed until all is combined.

Step 4: Pour the batter into the baking tray. Bake for about 40 minutes or until a wooden skewer comes out clean.

Step 5: Place on a cooling rack and let it cool for an hour. Decorate with decorating tools before serving. *(Optional)*

Almond Flour Banana Bread will keep for a week in a fridge or one month in a freezer.

Almond Flour Coconut Bread

INGREDIENTS:

2 cups **Almond Flour**

1 cups **Coconut Flour**

1 cup **Apple Puree**

½ cup **Almond Milk**

¼ cup **Honey**, raw

¼ cup **Olive Oil**, virgin, first cold pressed

4 tablespoons **Water**, hot

2 tablespoons **Flax Seeds**, ground

1 teaspoon **Baking Soda**

1 teaspoon **Vanilla**, extract, pure

¼ teaspoon **Salt,** fine, pink, Himalayan

Cooking Spray for greasing the baking tray

EQUIPMENT:

Rectangular bread baking tray, Stand or hand mixer fitted with the paddle attachment, Measuring cups, Cup, Fork, Wire cooling racks, Parchment paper (optional), Cake decorating piping tips and bags (optional).

PREPARATION:

Step 1: Prepare egg replacement: add flax seeds into a cup and cover it with hot water. Place flax seeds onto a countertop and wait until flax seeds become gelatin-like.

Step 2: Grease the bottom and sides of the baking tray with a cooking spray. Line the bottom of the tray with parchment paper (optional).

Step 3: In a bowl of a stand mixer add apple puree, flax eggs, almond flour, coconut flour, almond milk, olive oil, honey, baking soda, salt, and vanilla extract. Process everything on low-medium speed until all is combined.

Step 4: Pour the batter into the baking tray. Bake for about 40 minutes or until a wooden skewer comes out clean.

Step 5: Place on a cooling rack and let it cool for an hour. Decorate with decorating tools before serving. *(Optional)*

Almond Flour Coconut Bread will keep for a week in a fridge or one month in a freezer.

Almond Flour Pumpkin Bread

INGREDIENTS:

2 cups **Almond Flour**

½ cup **Coconut Flour**

1 cup **Pumpkin**, puree

½ cup **Almond Milk**

¼ cup **Honey**, raw

¼ cup **Olive Oil**, virgin, first cold pressed

4 tablespoons **Water**, hot

2 tablespoons **Flax Seeds**, ground

1 teaspoon **Baking Soda**

1 teaspoon **Vanilla**, extract, pure

½ teaspoon **Pumpkin Pie Spice**

½ teaspoon **Cinnamon,** powder

¼ teaspoon **Salt,** fine, pink, Himalayan

Cooking Spray for greasing the baking tray

EQUIPMENT:

Rectangular bread baking tray, Stand or hand mixer fitted with the paddle attachment, Measuring cups, Cup, Fork, Wire cooling racks, Parchment paper (optional), Cake decorating piping tips and bags (optional).

PREPARATION:

Preheat the oven to 365°F.

Step 1: Cut the raw pumpkin, remove the seeds.

Place pumpkin pieces onto a baking tray. Bake the pumpkin for approximately forty minutes until it is soft. Set aside to cool. Place cooled pumpkin into the food processor. Process until smooth. Set aside.

Step 2: Prepare egg replacement: add flax seeds into a cup and cover it with hot water. Place flax seeds onto a countertop and wait until flax seeds become gelatin-like.

Alternatively, you can use 3-4 eggs.

Step 3: Preheat the oven to 355°F. Grease bottom and sides of the baking tray with a cooking spray. Line the bottom of the tray with parchment paper (optional).

Step 4: In a bowl add flax eggs, pumpkin puree, almond flour, coconut flour, almond milk, honey, olive oil, baking soda, salt, and spices. Process everything on low-medium speed until all is combined.

Step 5: Pour the batter into the baking tray. Bake for about 40 minutes or until a wooden skewer comes out clean.

Step 6: Place on a cooling rack and let it cool for an hour. Decorate with decorating tools before serving. *(Optional)*

Banana Flour Pumpkin Bread will keep for a week in a fridge or one month in a freezer.

Coconut Flour Banana Bread

INGREDIENTS:

3 cups **Coconut Flour**

2 **Bananas**, ripe, mashed

3 cups **Coconut Milk**

¼ cup **Honey**, raw

¼ cup **Olive Oil**, virgin, first cold pressed

1 teaspoon **Baking Soda**

1 teaspoon **Vanilla**, extract, pure

¼ teaspoon **Salt,** fine, pink, Himalayan

Cooking Spray for greasing the baking tray

For Flaxseed Egg:

4 tablespoons **Water**, hot

2 tablespoons **Flax Seeds**, ground

EQUIPMENT:

Rectangular bread baking tray, Stand or hand mixer fitted with the paddle attachment, Measuring cups, Cup, Fork, Wire cooling racks, Parchment paper (optional), Cake decorating piping tips and bags (optional).

PREPARATION:

Step 1: Prepare egg replacement: add flax seeds into a cup and cover it with hot water. Place flax seeds onto a countertop and wait until flax seeds become gelatin-like.

Step 2: Preheat the oven to 355°F. With a cooking spray grease the bottom and sides of the baking tray. Line the bottoms of the tray with parchment paper (optional).

Step 3: In a bowl of a stand mixer, mash bananas with a fork. Add flax eggs, coconut flour, olive oil, coconut milk, honey, baking soda, salt, and vanilla extract. Process everything on low-medium speed until all is combined.

Step 4: Pour the batter into the baking tray. Bake for about 40 minutes or until a wooden skewer comes out clean.

Step 5: Place on a cooling rack and let it cool for an hour. Decorate with decorating tools before serving. *(Optional)*

Coconut Flour Banana Bread will keep for a week in a fridge or one month in a freezer.

Coconut Flour Pumpkin Bread

INGREDIENTS:

2 cups **Coconut Flour**

1 ¾ cups **Coconut Milk**

½ cup **Coconut Flour**

1 cup **Pumpkin**, puree

¼ cup **Honey**, raw

¼ cup **Olive Oil**, virgin, first cold pressed

1 teaspoon **Baking Soda**

1 teaspoon **Vanilla**, extract, pure

½ teaspoon **Pumpkin Pie Spice**

½ teaspoon **Cinnamon,** powder

¼ teaspoon **Salt,** fine, pink, Himalayan

For Flaxseed Egg:

4 tablespoons **Water**, hot

2 tablespoons **Flax Seeds**, ground

Cooking Spray for greasing the baking tray

EQUIPMENT:

Rectangular bread baking tray, Stand or hand mixer fitted with the paddle attachment, Measuring cups, Cup, Fork, Wire cooling racks, Parchment paper (optional), Cake decorating piping tips and bags (optional).

PREPARATION:

Preheat the oven to 365°F.

Step 1: Cut pumpkin in half and remove the seeds. Cut pumpkin on pieces. Spray the baking tray with a cooking spray. Place pumpkin pieces onto the baking tray. Bake for approximately 40 minutes until pumpkin becomes soft. Set aside to cool.

Step 2: Place cooled pumpkin into the food processor. Process until smooth. Set aside.

Step 3: Prepare egg replacement: add flax seeds into a cup and cover it with hot water. Place flax seeds onto a countertop and wait until flax seeds become gelatin-like.

Alternatively, you can use 3-4 eggs.

Step 4: Preheat the oven to 355°F. Grease the bottom and sides of the baking tray with the cooking spray. Line the bottom of the tray with parchment paper (optional).

Step 5: In a bowl of stand mixer equipped with the paddle attachment add flax eggs, pumpkin puree, coconut flour, coconut flour, coconut milk, honey, baking soda, salt, and spices. Process everything on low-medium speed until all is combined.

Step 6: Pour the batter into the bread baking tray. Bake for about 40 minutes or until a wooden skewer comes out clean.

Step 7: Place on a cooling rack and let it cool for an hour. Decorate with decorating tools before serving. *(Optional)*

Coconut Flour Pumpkin Bread will keep for a week in a fridge or one month in a freezer.

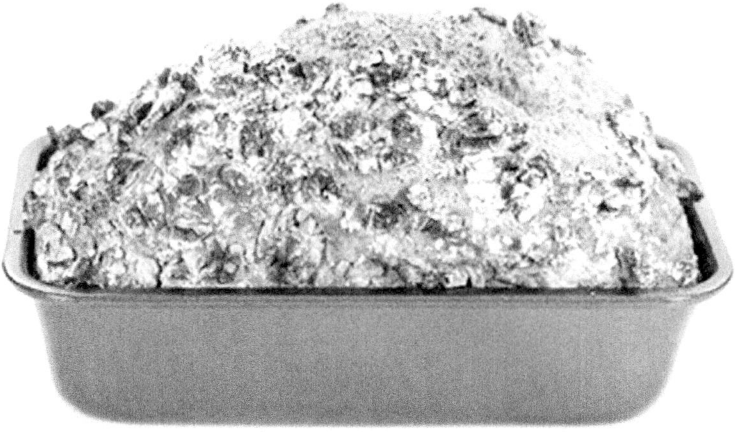

Thank You for Purchasing This Book!

I create and test recipes for you. I hope you enjoyed these recipes.

Your review of this book helps me succeed & grow. If you enjoyed this book, please leave me a short (1-2 sentence) review on Amazon.

Thank you so much for reviewing this book!

Do you have any questions?
Email me at: **Maria@BRILLIANTkithenideas.com**

MARIA SOBININA
BRILLIANT kitchen ideas

Would you like to learn cooking techniques and tips?
Visit us at:

www. BRILLIANTkitchenideas.com

Printed in Great Britain
by Amazon